Contra Mortem

a poetry sequence

E.M. Schorb

Copyright© 2019 E.M. Schorb
ISBN: 978-93-90202-03-4

First Edition: 2020
Rs. 200/-

Cyberwit.net
HIG 45 Kaushambi Kunj, Kalindipuram
Allahabad - 211011 (U.P.) India
http://www.cyberwit.net
Tel: +(91) 9415091004 +(91) (532) 2552257
E-mail: info@cyberwit.net

No part of this book may be reproduced or transmitted in any form or by any means, electronic, mechanical, photocopying, or otherwise, without the express written consent of E.M. Schorb.

Printed in India.

ACKNOWLEDGEMENTS

Grateful acknowledgement is given to the following publications in which some of these poems first appeared:

Agenda (England), *The American Scholar, Antioch Review, The Arts Journal, Atlanta Review, The Baltimore Review, The Chariton Review, The Classical Outlook, The Comstock Review, Context South, Crab Orchard Review, Deronda Review* (Israel), *Dream International Quarterly, Frank* (France), *Free Lunch, Ginosko, The Great American Poetry Show, The Hudson Review, In Whatever Houses We May Visit,* (Anthology, American College of Physicians), *The Interpreter's House* (England), *The Iowa Review, The Kansas Quarterly, The Laurel Review, Measure, Meridian Anthology, The Milo Review, Naugatuck River Review, New Welsh Review, Nimrod, North American Review, OffCourse Literary Journal, Outposts* (England), *The Phoenix Rising From the Ashes,* (Anthology), *Poetry Salzburg Review, Poetry Super Highway, Princeton Arts Review, Private Photo Review, Raleigh News and Observer, The Sewanee Review, Shenandoah, The South Carolina Review, Southern Poetry Review, Sparrow '62, Spring: the Journal of the E.E. Cummings Society, Stand* (England), *The Tennessee Quarterly, Timber Creek Review, Verse, Verse Wisconsin, Virginia Quarterly Review, Voices Israel, War, Literature & the Arts, Wascana Review* (Canada), *Webster Review, Whiskey Island Magazine,* and *The Yale Review.*

Contents

IV

I

LEGAL

They stood in a cracked photograph before your tenth
birthday cake like puckered fountain cupids, helping you
to blow out your candles and in your wish. Your wish
then was that they would never grow old, a child's
wish, born of dependency, your need for them
to flourish for your sake. You looked away, about,
and wondered, if, upon your return to the mainland,
your parents would look the same as always, the same
as in the cracked photograph, or look old, altered.
You glanced up, and saw a long, black, tail-finned
limousine, shining moons of sun, pass out of
sight on the busy street where you entered the bar;
and, startled out of your reverie, you turned about
to find Waikiki Beach behind you, a keepsake
postcard of one of the most important days
of your life, and you wondered at the power
of your first legal drink to so disorient you;
for, when you entered, you were looking out at the sea.
Then you realized that you were on a turntable,
imperceptibly turning counterclockwise, but only,
of course, by the machinations of human will.

THE ROSES

The wishes live together in unease.
I see no stasis, but a perilous balance.
I watch as roses disassemble, petal
and petal, touched with darkened tips
and edges, and think of when they bloomed,
how determined their becoming,
how absolute. I have watched the gardens.
I have watched them carefully and long.

I think the wishes live together in unease.
Just when the turn comes, I'm not sure.
The roses hold and hold late in the year
but at some point surrender, at some point
you can't identify, it seems before you see it,
and you are looking, looking long and hard,
and then you realize that it has happened—
the roses wither, fall.

It's true that the wishes live together in unease:
the thing you knew was magic—you look again—
is just pedestrian. Is it because
you know more than you did, or have you lost
a knowledge you possessed? The wishes live
like twins who hate each other, jealous twins,
who want your only love. Live, says one, Die,
the other; and they stare across
your holy land like enemies, but finally
they compromise, and hold the ground they have.
And this can last most of a lifetime, like
the freshness of the rose that holds throughout
most of the summer and almost into winter.

THE SOULS

Outside on a green lawn a giant water-oak conducts a sunset.
   Some unsteady hum has summoned us out of our houses.
My ancient lady friend, who lives nearby, is jawing now, and wears
   an awed-holy expression as she says they are souls, yes sir.
And they are everywhere, they wade the dusky clouds, they are
   giant black-winged fruits hanging, falling, bouncing. The green
is black with them. And neighbors stare; they worry for their

cars and pickups. If they get into the red berries, it's hell on
   paint. Shoot them. No, they are beautiful. They are a menace.
Look out below! They rise and wheel, kaleidoscopic, inside rings
   of themselves. They set themselves against the sky, black on blue.
They caw. They are telling themselves, or us, something.
   They caw and caw, and what is it they are saying, so
earpiercingly, holes through your eardrums, through your brain,

as if lasered? Then they settle again, like a black blizzard
   of huge coal flakes. The souls come back to visit us, to tell
us that they know everything now. Now their sharp yellow beaks
   pierce the lawn. They are busier than worms, in a feast
of famishment, an ecstasy of appetite. Now, she says,
   the nonagenarian, I'll soon be with them, and then
it's always now for me like them. The souls have found their

bodies. I don't know which is which, but somewhere, there,
   is everyone who died, all the loved ones, and even the others,
the ones that nobody loved, they are all there now, she says.
   I stare as deep as I can see. They are every blessed
place—on roofs, looking down, in trees, on bushes, under,

over, and around. Some seem to be waiting, some tug
at the turning-emerald lawn in the lowering light: and now

how do they know to rise suddenly, and become one wide
    black wing? How do they know to circle and circle in unison,
one boomerang black wing composed of so many blood-beating,
    sky-rowing black wings? How do they know when it's time
to fly along a horizon, rimmed with rising red? The souls,
    they know, they know! I think it must be out of some distant
folklore that the old lady speaks, eyes fixed, waving them goodbye.

POSTCARD

You are growing old, & too sad for your own good, judging
by your last missive where you wrote that you were tired

of reading bad unrhyming *vers libre*, as you put it,
& newspaper headlines filled with murder & mayhem,

& that we humans are merely the slaves of all we survey,
meaning I take it the slaves of our impulses & not

the lords & owners of our faces as Shakespeare wrote
in one of those sonnets of his which you used to read

as others read the Bible, the Bible which you attribute to lesser poets
whose muse is a God in whom you do not believe.

Is it your loss of my proximity that has led you to this depression?
For you seem depressed & lonely, & I'm sorry I had to move away.

I had a family to care for & this distant spot served the purpose,
& now one child has a child & there are others here on the way.

See the photograph of the lake on the other side of this card—
it is beautiful here, but let me tell you something about it.

Out on the lake fishing the husband of the woman next door
was stung by a bee & died before he could dock.

He was a slave to the lake & the fish, I suppose,
if you are correct when you say we are slaves to all we survey.

The bee must have been a slave to the man in the boat
since he got close enough to lose his stinger to him.

But I am also writing with reference to unrhyming Kilroy
whom you deplore & who has just won the Nobel Prize.

Actually Kilroy writes both with rhyme and without
as did Shakespeare & Whitman ("O Captain! My Captain!") & Frost.

Even now I am writing you an unrhyming poem called "To a Sad Friend."
Why not come & visit me—we can go out & fish on the lake.

The fish & the bees can survey us & be our bright slaves
& I'll do my best to cheer you up about Kilroy

& meaningless unrhyming poems & mayhem & murder.
You can look at the children & see there is some good in life.

ROANOKE RETURN

Six-hundred miles above my southern exposure
my friend in extremis waits,
a man old enough to be my father,
and I am heading up North Carolina
in the long heartless dark,
to big, bad, only-the-dead-know Brooklyn,
headlights blazing on high beams,
being blinked at, warned and horned
—for I am faring to where one half
of my split spirit dies, in my war hero
drinking buddy, Elbert, two silver stars,
two purple hearts, smiling up ahead of me,
wan smile of age: Normandy's gone.

Tarheeled, tarwheeled, I wend my way,
blinking lights stream-ing into my brain,
to Brooklyn, that Elbert calls God's,
over hills of North Carolina night,
knowing the running greens and pines along the road,
how they set themselves against the running moon,
in my camouflaged combat jumpsuit
big enough for Santa jumping Claus,
soaked through with unholdable brew,
while the moon swings. . . the two moons
. . . and Elbert swings. . . in and out. . .
of the Fort Hamilton Veteran's Hospital
with his lungs smoked away, brave as ever—
Elbert, I give you a new medal,
the moon, the two moons, one for each

black lung—we will jag together once again
in your unbelieved-in-God's country,
where you might be looking at the moon, too.

It is a mad quest of hope and love
up 77 to Roanoke, link up with 85,
smooth over-drive to Harrisburg,
up the night to Jersey, climbing up,
up the great flying sky-harp cathedral Verrazano
and dumped at your Fort Hamilton feet—
Elbert, I salute you!

My olive-drab seabag bounces in back
like a wild love pregnant with burning vodka
and cheap-at-the-source Carolina cigs, deadly
gifts Elbert begged me to bring, only sooner,
in time for us to enjoy them together,
a lifetime of death brought now
and become magic to stop him from dying,
burning and unburnt offerings!
. . . in and out of smoking clouds,
lightnings, with the moon in and out,
escaping, seeking, avoiding love, age,
death, my wife, children, responsibilities
that begin in dreams. . . waves of water,
wind pressing me across lane lines,
and I am in the fast lane, pulling
around a slow-climbing eighteen-wheeler
honking like a tug, beaming me down,
wet speed and mild madness streaming away behind me.
It is a hot shower in a Roanoke motel room
and a nightmaring, dream-drunken sleep.
It is black coffee and a long-distance call,
and it is all too late, for me, for Elbert,

Officialdom now in charge of his skinny bones
—I hoped the metastasizing crab broke its teeth
on the embedded shrapnel that for fifty years
stabbed out through his skin in bloody stigmata
—and it is the long sad hungover journey home
in a day dark as night and relentless rain
falling down Virginia, North Carolina,
it is "Pardon me, boy. . ."
on the static-stuttering radio,
blanking, blanking out in the low country,
and it is the wrong rainy road, ascending. . .
looking out at water-colored what?
A Wailing Wall of water—
and I am high and outside, low and inside,
denim-backed white-duck fog and no lights, no cars,
no world but rain, alone, blood-shot eyes cotton-blind,
gearing up and down, burning brakes, clutch,
going round the side of something big
—the wet rockface of a Great Smoky,
with the steaming abyss of eternity below.
Elbert the Brave, be here as I quake,
strengthen me, breathless, on high,
going down, down down down too fast,
I dip, I spin, I slide, I am sideways,
backwards, tottering at a precipice
facing the past, rocking, rocking, stopped.
I am in heaven with nothing but down on one side,
hungover, scared—ALIVE—with the land down under
wet blue and green between -layers of stranding smoke,
money in fog banks, and I pull off, away
from one possible end, sidestepping death.
All praise to Elbert, I am steady.
Love, I will be home tonight!

LOOKING DOWN AT A FRIEND

for Patrick, R.I.P.

Always, now, truth is the tight suit that you wear.
You twirl your diamonded cane as you dance in stillness.
Forever takes you no time at all, so you can't
be expected to wait for those who loved you, slow
alive and grieving unlike your fast asleep self
playing on the moon, transported everywhere at once.
Friend, you seem not to miss your old friends, you
seem to be busy elsewhere, unfaithful seeker.

Dare you not remember those who loved you? Dare you?
Whom you have caused such suffering? What do you seek,
now, in the no-wind wind, in the no-place place
where nothing is most powerfully itself?
Lying there, where are you going with your stolen self?
You were always one on a journey somewhere, even when still.

DESTRUCTION

In Florida a hurricane
came off the sea and
razed the town of
Homestead, in which
town lived a little
boy—in a mobile home,
a singlewide, on wheels—
whose hobby it was, he
told the reporter,
to build houses out of
cards. His mother worked,
his father had died, he
had no sister or brother,
no other, so when he came
home from school, second
grade, he would stack
cards, most beautifully,
the reporter gathered, up and up
and into the most wonderful
designs, so wonderful, he
said, that his mother
had photographed some of
his houses made of cards
(but the photos had been
blown away by the storm—
as well as everything else).
The boy said he could
stack some more, and
didn't care, his talent

remained, but frowned
and said, in a small voice,
that he felt sorry
for the wind.

FLASHBACKS

You are doing something thoroughly mundane one day,
say, peeling carrots, and you are suddenly where
you once were while your hands go on with their work
and you are staring into the sun from under a shed
roof, where you and your other are arguing over
what you have done and now you remember that part,
the part of it that was about what you had done:
then you are wondering why you did it, what
ever possessed you to do such a stupid thing,
and it occurs to you as it has in a past you've
almost forgotten that you might have been arrested
for doing such a thing and no wonder that you and
your other argued over it, how could it have been
otherwise?
       Of course it was a terrible mistake
to have made: it was a wonder that your other stayed
with you, who had done such a thing, but in the shed
in the last light of evening you finally made up and
even now you experience the sweetness of the kiss
of forgiveness as if it were warming your lips as you
peel the last of the carrots and you remember what
you are supposed to be doing though it is difficult
to draw away from that moment in the sunset shed
that seems somehow to be happening as you stand
where you are: but then you realize that you have cut
yourself and are bleeding. You must bandage your finger.
You must wash the carrots and cook them. You must not
forget this event, you think, as you have so many others.

NO ANGEL

Because you are you

& because they do not suffer
because their weather is never harsh
& they share nothing of the storms
that drive us in and burn us out
& because they are never in trouble
because they do not dance but on a pin
because they have no heat for anger
because they have no blood because
they do not eat drink nor defecate
& because they have no sense of humor
& because their lips are not discernable
but for a wide thin crease from ear to ear
& because their eyes are empty
but for the expansive light of heaven
& because they have not heard of sex
because they are never lonely
& because they do not judge
because they are not human
because they are abstract
& because their bodies are illusion
& because their wings beat nothing
& because they have no will but God's

you are higher than the angels

Where Are You?

What life does to us
is strange, too strange,
I suppose, for many to
think about. But I
think about it, about
how you were here,
right here with the
rest of us, and now
are not, are gone into
the ground and maybe
are waving in the grass,
or are sitting silent
there, being the rock,
or are looming up
and reaching out,
being the tree, or are
drifting easily down
the street, being
the leaves burning
and the smoke.

Where are you?
You cannot not be anywhere.
I want you to come back;
but you can't, I know.
I can fan the air
with my hands and
do no good. I was
sitting here, right here,

with you, and you were
saying or doing something
and I was not attending,
I was thinking my own
thoughts, but what
are they now? I
should have listened
deeply to you. I
should have recorded
your voice in my mind,
so that I could hear you
again and again until
I myself am smoke.

HOUDINI AND THE DYING SWAN

Where was he? Was it a tunnel?
But he had come to a wall,
a slimy, wormy wall.
He must break through.
He must break out.
He felt for a tool.

Naked, she lay back in the tub,
white as a white swan, long-necked
as a swan, thin as a silken thread,
her gloriously thick dark hair
piled loosely up, collapsing
onto her wide, sloping shoulders,
dark, water-dipped ringlets forming,
her swan's-down skin pinking,
steam misting her swan song,
her suicide with water and razor.

II

They concentrated. A glittering
company. Rich. Celebrated.
They waited for the great Houdini.
His monument was dark, unmoving.
The stars glittered, like the company.
Half a minute. They breathed
in short, shuddering breaths,
and waited. Houdini heard:
"Houdini, do not disappoint us,
for we must believe that Death
cannot take us, utterly."

Tearing at the wall, his long
yellow fingernails cracked off,
ricocheted; then he heard:
"I am dying, dying . . ." He drew back,
prepared to throw his body at the wall
—*he* must *break through . . .*

III

The steaming water in the marble tub
was streaked in ribbons of red.
She was going to die, that *he* would know,
her lover, what he had done.
He had killed beauty
in neglect and pursuit of money.
He would be sorry. Her long lashes locked.
It was like a dream, and she was falling,
falling over a dark sea, which now she struck.
The noise jolted her. It was like
breaking plaster, like tumbling bricks,
like an earthquake. Her eyelids rolled back
to see a mad-eyed specter
emerge from a great, gaping hole
torn through tiles. Her dizzy mind,
half-bloodless, saw the bloodless form,
and fainted. Houdini lifted her from
the marble tub and taped her wrists.
He put her in her bed and tugged
the bell pull. She was too beautiful to die.
A great grandfather clock obliterated
the last of midnight. A doorknob turned,
and he went back the way that he had come.

Houdini darkened into death.

DEATH ROW

In the Prison of the North,
in some Bismarck of winter,
the bars are ice, the walls
are iceberg tips, and the guards
steer past the cells on sleds of frozen water.
Whiteness at night, with shadows
behind each corner: thin cotton blankets
to teach us a lesson, another lesson,
one more than all the others.
But Death Row is not a place,
anymore than Purgatory,
it's a waiting period, and we stand
naked in it until, frozen, we fall,
we fall and break, we shatter,
we grit the floor like rice.
Fire here is the touch of ice—
we light our mentholated cigarettes
with a touch of ice, with our own fingertips,
our lost and blackened and found-again toes.
We light our smokes with our frost-bitten,
blackened toes and watch white paper
burning back, turning black, and a red spark
with its dark smoke vanish in the winter light.
This is what we get for being what we are—
monsters with ice-water in our veins,
cold-blooded killers of love, runaways.
The prison of the North does not contain us,
we contain it, got it young, most of us,
got it and walk about with it freezing up

inside us, got it and can't find warmth,
don't remember how, and the worst
of it is that we cannot even touch
one another or we shatter. Do you hear
that creaking sound? One of us
has tried to touch another,
the oh-so-lonely one we call
The Refrigerator, has tried to find a friend,
the friend he tried to find we call The Freezer.
The Refrigerator sought love so savagely
that he was iced in love's bipolar cell,
and now his durance on Death Row is done.

DEATH

What do I know about death?
It is a question one must
occasionally ask oneself
Death who are you what are you
No metaphor will do
because that is merely
a likening of one thing
to another thing, which
when it comes to death
is impossible, for
death being unknown
anything we should
choose would be
arbitrarily chosen
and therefore
would be a bad
metaphor nobody
being able to say
how close or distant
the vehicle
from the tenor
the subject being
death. How then
do we approach this
unsubject this
antisubject this
but you see
even here
is a metaphor

 E.M. Schorb

even here
we are at a loss
that we are asking
a question for which
the only answer
is death.

THE BOSNIAN CHERRY

> *. . . the explosion appears to have*
> *shocked the tree into blossom.*
>   *—Reuters*

Friends, look with faithless unbelieving eyes
upon this miracle the bomb has wrought,
as now, in shocked conversion, I tell you
of spring against the devastated skies
of winter war, the hopelessness war brought,
and how, enveloped in explosive blue
of acrid smoke, this tree could still devise
beyond predictability. It caught
the shell's enormous heat, and grew
fluid with sap, miraculous with surprise
of spring, for all combatants to be taught
anew a faith unlearned by deathly cries,
a blossoming the human heart has sought
with every hopeful spring—a sweet-peace prize.

AN EVENING WITH "BLOOD"

Art, being bartender, is never drunk;
And magic that believes itself, must die. . .
                              —Peter Viereck

Just call when you hit town, the great man wrote.
I like your work, and we must talk about it.
He lived one red state down, an hour's drive,
and I had business there. I called him up,
and he invited us to "Come right out,"
to hurry to his house, "and help me drink
a quart of Southern Comfort that a student
of mine has given me—I need some help.
Today above all days I need some help—
a falling down, and then a falling out!
How soon?" he asked. "As soon as we can get there."
The bard swayed hugely at his door to greet us.
"I've got *your* names locked in. You call me Blood.
It was my nickname when I was a kid.
I like your husband's work," he told my wife.
"It's very individual—which I,
and Emerson, and Wallace Stevens, think
is most important. Possum doesn't, though,
but he is wrong." The lakeside house was empty
but for the three of us, a huge TV—
the N.F.L. in combat filled the screen—
and roaring fans and players, who loomed large.
"It's an old game. I like to run the plays
and second guess with twenty-twenty hindsight.
I tore your poems apart like that and found

I couldn't take much out—that's good!
Don't write, re-write! I drop them and go back.
This took five years—to make a wall of words
stand up like that. I worked spasmodically.
The novel took ten years, but it was worth it.
It brought a lot of money, and the movie,
and the chance for me to play a part myself.
That's Blood up on the screen, that character.
He'd scare the shit out of you, wouldn't he?
That wasn't acting, that was really me.
You see this arrow? Penetrate skull-bone.
Know how to use a crossbow? Here, I'll show you.
Up—like that—that's right. Now you aim and fire.
Bring down a rhino, that thing would. But Blood
says that you need another drink, and then
I'll play the banjo for you. Read me this one—
the one about the mad marine. I *love* it,"
he told my wife. "I love the really mad ones.
Did you see how I got myself arrested?
Drunk driving. What I do is brownbag out
into the woods and turn my highbeams on
and try to see above them, not the helmet
of ordinary life down here. You too?
We yearn for levitation, flights of fancy.
I flew a lot of missions in the war.
Yes, Blood has done a major share of burning,
incendiaried towns and populations,
and no one ever understands you right
again when you've done that. My explanation
is in my poetry for those with guts to know.
As for the rest, I cannot help the world.
Above the high beams is the zodiac.
Let fools ask there about this fire-bombed world.
Blood's in the dark—like him—like you, sweet lady."

THE ISLANDS OF LANGERHANS

Islands of Langerhans—
scattered cell groups in the
pancreas which produce insulin

Stream of consciousness, WWII Veteran,
Hospitalized, diabetic, dying. .

in memory of an uncle

Woke once to
white-smocked aliens
their poetic rap
the crystalline
active principle of
the Islands of Langerhans
insulin
palm trees swaying
ukulele music
sarongs
Hollywood presents the
Islands of Langerhans
with Boris Karloff
as Langerhans
the mad scientist who invites
the alien pod people to land
and institutional footsteps
down the hollow hall
hollow footsteps down
hollow footsteps
in an echo chamber

Silver Hollows near the sea
ukulele music
on the crystalline
Islands of Langerhans
emerald islands
in a crystalline sea
in Oceanside in
Golden Land
Silver Hollows
in Golden Land
near the sea
where you can see
the Islands of Langerhans
in an echo
of crystalline footsteps
down a hollow hall
where white-smocked aliens
rap poetically
where you forgot to take
your insulin
you know you can go
into sugar shock or
insulin shock
if you don't take care of
your only friend
and you like a kid
have to spend all day
at Disneyland
eating cake and candy
and swilling beer
unbalanced
Disneyland in Golden Land
Hollywood

sarongs
ukulele music
palm trees swaying
the Islands of Langerhans
their crystalline
active principle
poetic rap of the
white-smocked aliens
who took samples
of your blood
on a raised white table

The beach at Langerhans
is heavily fortified
and there's a rough surf
many died
before they hit the beach
awarded the Purple Elvis
        and the Flying Saucer
        for the bullet plugged in
        at the neck
        and drove down
        and out through the ribs
        under the right arm
        rapping he'll be out of it
        in a day or two
        rebalance of sugar-insulin
        treat as shock
        then nothing but
        the white-smocked aliens
        who landed at Langerhans
        I was afraid
        when I saw them

>   they echo'd and echo'd
>   down the long hallways
a Silver Hollows sound
but they will transfer me
to a VA hospital
heard their crystalline
poetic rap
footsteps
echoing down
wasn't afraid of God's
musical castle
wasn't afraid at all
because old was young
when we hit the beach
at Langerhans at
not Langerhans
at Normandy

A REPLY

When the wind blows down the house we thank the Lord
    that we were out that day; or, when the sea
turns our mast under its swashing opaque belly,
    and we are thrown clear, we swim and pray
thanksgiving, thanksgiving, selfishly forgetting
    that, like so many bits of bait, our brothers
twirl downward in the darkness, being bitten and consumed
    —but when you say you are an atheist,
then qualify that you're a rationalist as well,
    you say to me your reason's on vacation.

For all we know, there *is* a God, a chemist,
    and we are the byproducts of experiment,
luckily unknown to the great creator,
    who, if that creator were to learn of us,
might draw from a vast laboratory a sterilizer
    and spray us from the surface of the earth.

We don't know what or why we are, my epistolary friend,
    only that we are and we can think,
and with this small equipment we can challenge existence,
    that it not best us for a time, at least.
For each of us can triumph for a time, even the unborn
    has spent some positive force in first
dividing against the inertia of matter, a tiny Knight
    against the Dragon of Death, or unaliveness,
a dust adumbrating itself against the odds.

A HUNDRED YEARS

Although the sea won't pose,
the picture that the boardwalk takes is clear.
In each ear, the old man says, he has a baby mouse
that squeals sometimes and makes the surf high-pitched.
A hundred years of being here, he says,
seems merely like a day, a day with many nights.
Once, he kept the old lighthouse, once, a tackle shop,
and once he was a fisherman himself, also selectman once,
but then he laughs and says he married twice.
Most of the Earth, he says, is sea,
most of a man is water,
and mother comes from *mare* and *meer* and others,
the sea we swim before our birth.
Once, too, he was a farmer,
and calved the cows inland, but not for long.
The sea must call him back, he must have the sea,
or the sea have him.
In a hundred years you learn a thing or two,
he says, but not so much as you might think.
Mostly it's the magic of it all.
You are born with that, you have that right away,
but then there's sex, and then there's all
that business in between that's meant to keep us going,
the race I mean, and you forget the magic
in the business, the busyness, he adds,
and you work hard, and you are tired a lot, and only see
     the sea,
as with your mind and not that sense the youngest have
that's gained again in age, when time's more free,

and you can feel the flow of life right on your skin.
You feel the wind, now, I don't doubt, but do you feel
the other thing? Do you feel the secret thing?
Do you feel the thing behind the wind?
Aldebaran was so bright last night,
I 'most could take it in my hand,
not so simple as a jewel, but a spiritual thing.
When I look at the sea, or at the stars at night,
I do not fear my hundred years as you might think.
They do not wish to go or stay.
They are always here with you and everything.

AND/OR

variations on a theme

1/The Invocation

I lean forward
feel my body
but become
my mind
soul
doing bidding
informed
to do
each does
must do
be
tran
scribing
in gregg
pitman
keeping
track
keeping
up
with
dictator
fired
for art
listen
the poem

is on
the way
thank
AND the
bugles
blow
in the
OR world

2/The Contemplation

AND
is making
what
AND knows
not OR

OR knows
what OR
makes
OR makes
what AND
knows
AND is
making

I make
this on a
field of
action
as I am

told by
my making
mind
AND's

can AND
make a
mistake
AND makes
everything
is OR's
best an
swer no
pangloss
served here
quack

3/Quark

an
atom
charging
angrily
around
is never trying
to find a place
to light
for it
getting there
is all the fun
the relatives

will be boring
its friends forgotten
atom doesn't care
it's a dare
a dare
let me go there
AND there
AND there
more AND
more
AND
atom
get hotter AND
hotter
barely holding
its particles
together
looping around
its own light
around AND
around
pulling away
from the pull
of its own
gravity
elliptical
like a man
with a beer
belly
then
thin again
so fast
in such a hurry

to be
where
it's
in
scape
heartbeating out
ballooning
shaking
shining
shooting
rocketing off
OR
barking
wagging
hissing
OR
knifing up
green through soil
pressing
in in
visible
no-stas
is to
renaissance
budding
blooming
blossoming
bursting
blowing out
up away
AND
starting again

AND again
AND again
heart pounds
head thumps
brain
pulses
communicating
message received
before sent
it seems
ions
zip zap
where's
time
here
see the
labanotation
of bird feet
in mud they
dance now
still as
they fly
away
see
the muddy
dance
see

AND see
them flying
being OR in
AND

it is all on the field
I feel it
the boy fielded the ball
how he felt when it hit his glove
it was like light
like love

like ein's
grace

4/Envoi

gert
stein
sd
prose
is telling
poetry
naming
adamic
naming
a tree
a snake
parvis
parvis

AND
help me
I am
but an
OR

OLD WOMEN, PAUSING

Old women, pausing, standing midblock on a hill
or midlevel on subway steps, waiting for breath,
their shopping bags hanging from toughened hands,
their eyes back in girlhood, perhaps, or ahead,
on the next meal, the contents of the bags
cooked and served, their honor again earned,
exist away from where they are, the grade or incline
slowly flattening, reversing, as their hearts calm
and their breath comes slower, more peacefully;
and so they stand, with the stillness of statues,
black-coated, black-shod, eyes straight ahead,
wisps of pale hair riffling slightly with the breeze,
waiting for breath, ahead of or behind where they are.
—So all of us, ahead of or behind where we are
or separated from what we are, not complete,
having left part of ourselves behind,
not having done that which we hoped to do,
not having attained to that which we hoped to attain,
all like old women, standing midblock on a hill,
waiting for breath, ahead of or behind where we are.

THE NURSING HOME

There are more women than
men in the nursing home and
more men than old doctors.

Staff doctors visit once a
month. The few old men do
very little but sleep. Two

or three of them occasionally
gather outside in clear
weather for a smoke, which

is allowed them. I suppose
those in charge feel that
it can make no difference

now, and it brings the old
men a little pleasure. I
sit and chat with them

sometimes. Perhaps "chat"
is a bit too lively a word
to describe what passes for

conversation during these
puffing sessions. A lot
of low grunting goes on.

There is one old man who
is afflicted with bone
cancer and who says, in

high good humor, that his
guarantees have run out.
He was a travelling salesman

in women's wear, and still
remembers how much he loved
women. Many of the women

have become little girls
again. They carry dolls
about with them, mostly

rag-dolls, I suppose so
they can't injure themselves
when they squeeze them.

To see these toothless,
balding old ladies, frail
as twigs, clutching these dolls,

is heartbreaking. Oh, to love
something! It's still there.
It has been in them since

they were little and had dirty
knees and bows in their hair.
Some recognize me now, and,

when I give them a wave,
they wave back. It's a
wonderful feeling to make

contact, but it is difficult
to tell how much they know.
The care-givers are kind and

efficient. They are mostly
young, and apparently try
to imbue the old with some of

their zest for life, but
of course the old know all
that already—or knew and have

forgotten it. I wonder,
can the young reverse their
situations with the old

and see themselves looking up
at such fresh faces from the
vantage of bed or wheelchair

or walker? I am too young
to join the old here in the
nursing home, this metaphor

(or is it the tenor of a
metaphor?) for the last days,
but I am too old

to feel the buoyancy of the
young; so, at least for the
context of the nursing home,

I have arrived at yet another
awkward age. After visiting
my mother, who is only partly

present, I go out and sit
with the old men and have a
smoke. We hope for clear days.

THE LOSS

When the blackbird stood on the chimney and called,
poking her beak at the clear blue ice of the sky,
I watched from inside the frame of an old wooden house
across from the once two-chimneyed house where she stood,
heard her cry crack the ice of the sky that day
from the wrongest of chimneys, the wrongest.
The bricks lay scattered next to the house.
The big nest of hay had blown away.
The ugly babies now lived in the barn,
but for one, who had drowned in the well.

LEADBELLY

for the musical ghost of Blind Lemon Jefferson

> Leadbelly, grim with your Cajun accordion,
> with your harmonica blues, with your knife
>   flicking down the twelve strings of your guitar
>   *—the Rock Island Line was a mighty good road—*
>   bowing, scraping, white-suited trainman . . .
> made your pride sick, but you sang,
>   fast, strong, quiet, like a driven
> demon, like you had to get it out
>   before a razor dumped your guts
> on a blood-mud taphouse floor,
>   or some drunk crazy rednecks
> nailed you up like Christ, in a dangerous world
>   for anybody but most America for a black
> poet of low-down places and sky-high loves.
>
> Leadbelly, thirty years hard time murder,
>   six and a half, sang your way out, ten more, intent,
>   then Alan Lomax and his bro, John, folklorists—
> makes you laugh inside at night—white boys,
>   playing—but they get you out again and in
> the Library of Congress, that grinding
>   voice part now of something big, like
> storm darkness, like that lifething,
>   love, always beyond somewhere or
> crying deep inside, in a dark place,
>   yeah, big like music, big like that gal you
> call Irene! How many Irenes, you think?

Even the Lomax bros, even them white boys,
they know Irene—you driving them through
   New York traffic, them folkloring in back and you
being their folkloring black chauffeur.
   You drink sharp liquor in Harlem, play
with Woody Guthrie, Sonny Terry, Brownie
   McGhee, the Headline Singers—radio too,
   Hollywood and *Three Songs by Leadbelly,*
      a French tour . . . . You show 'em your razor
stretch marks, your shotpitted pot.
      Good night Irene I'll see you in my dreams . . .
all that good hot mean hard American life
      and Lou Gehrig's *amyotrophic lateral sclerosis.*
   It's *The Midnight Special*!   Fade me, Death!

ELEGY

This compass-headed bird,
     dead-reckoning South in Fall,
arcing its bloody breast
     above the roof and cawing
some kind of bold farewell
     to higher air and leaderless
V'd fliers off on it,
     was shot (we saw and heard),
and staggered in the sky,
     dripping blood and guts
down on the lobstered roofers
     working in the sun.
It sang its downfall swan
     song silently, now, spread
its wings, and then, as silent
     as its eyes, it lay
resting on the roof,
     face up, and looked at clouds,
(and some sweet heaven we
     could almost see); but soon
pain shook it like an angry
     nurse, so one good roofer
struck head from body with
     a spade, merciful severance,
and catwalked off, bloody
     spade dragging on the tiles,
a man of dirty duty,
     unlike the murderer

of song, the wanton boy-
                    in-man, who pellet-shot
the bird (the shot we heard);
                    and this once musical,
most bright and beautiful,
                    small dust was part of all.

ANTHOLOGIES ARE SAD

Impressed by smoking-ember music,
as I have always been, drinking gin,
and reading the poets of the past—
who are in anachronistic pain
as if alive, striving, thriving
today—I think of today's.

I have a new anthology,
one including me,
with, alas, dates.
Most have only births and dashes,
a few the flying ashes,
the smoking music, of the past—
dates that say, *At last! At last!*

What then of Berryman
and those other merry men
and women who were human—
in pain and joy—alive?
In the anthologies they thrive,
possessing their due dates!

So now I turn a page,
afraid to find my final age;
and, though my last is but a dash,
I feel the flutter of ash.

NEWS OF 45

Into his mid-life crisis
desperate man stalks wild
life brings home head of
thought for wall display
mounting it for worship
plenty yet more to come
proudly shows it to friends
who scoff saying some
body else got it for you
like hell they did shot
gun see all the holes
in it but its mine mine
mine proud of it autumnal
macho laughable necessary
joy so worry not thy heart
days of glory upon thy
wrinkled brow sparks
of plenty more to come
next better yet which
could be worse who
knows but plunge on
plunge on with no effort
for light takes you
smilingly home as you
stay & practice your
declensions sun-o
moon-a your conju
gations selvesyes

selvesalways selves
before selvesafter
glory glory glory
for my five & forty.

MEMENTO MORI

When these blow-dried twigs
finally fall, or are deracinated,
tangled in some last, accomplished comb,
or in the glib fingers of a lover
fine-boned and sharp-nailed enough

to play tweezers, the scarred skin
will gleam nakedly in the mirror,
burnished by sun and overhead bulb
and, quick as life, we shall have been
transformed into a meditative monk,

skull-capped and burnoosed, who
belongs to the Monastery of Maturity,
and bears on his weary shoulders,
silently, to his last small cell,
his own *memento mori*.

THE NIGHT SWEATS

By our intensity, with hanging head,
we spell the wolf away, who pants and croons
outside the door, who wants us to be dead
so he may have his meal. By magic runes
we rid the world of wide-winged evil loons
whose madness mixes metaphors instead
of bringing clarity, whose looney tunes
make breathless nightmares in our sweat-wet bed.
Hear them who creep toward our peace of mind,
destructive artifices of our brains,
to wreak their havoc! Run, leave them behind!
And in the dark we try to run in chains
and can't escape because the night is mined
to blow us up in spite of all our pains.

DEATH AND THE MERMAID

This mermaid is a virgin,
dreaming her last dream,
her upper half human and
milk-breasted, with seaweed-
tangled but human hair,
not an elderly patient
on display in a cave of plastic,
hearing the susurrus of the sea
in her own harsh breath.
She kicks, kicks open
her blanket-bandaged,
fish-tailed lower half
in her bound dream,
as the second tide
smacks hard on the rocks
a mile from the sanitarium
and foams in. *Life*, she cries,
in a siren sound, *life, life,*
under her plastic hood,
but Death dreams back
with a huge, curlicue wave
and spindrift, and the
cave-water rises, floating her up
on her forked, fish tail, where
she stands, breasts floating,
dark, tangled hair sparkling with
water-jewels, and leans forward,
into the tide, away
from a woman's world

of men, and reaches her
glistening long arms out
to take in the rising sea,
her only lover at the end.

THE DIAMOND MERCHANT

A diamond is forever.
—B. J. Kidd

The buoys of memory have faint bells, noticed in the night.
I have left these chiming seamarks for the time of my return.
They ring out there, but faintly, so faintly I can hardly hear.
I think they want me to remember the severances of the soul,
if soul is more than mere electric tissue. If Death is king
and I do not reclaim what I have jettisoned, it goes to him.
I do not want the king to have my life. Therefore, each night at sea,
I must set out to find the ringing buoys and haul aboard
the lagan realities, for now my aging body, my emotional mal de mer,
lend renewed reality to the cold, damp camps. One numbered friend
should wear a wedding ring, another was engaged, and yet a third,
below and silent, had eyes like Tavernier blue diamonds set in Fabergé
eggshell by the master. I cannot put a name to the smiling face I see,
but she existed, who is now the faint dream of a denouement.

     Shalom alekhem   Shalom alekhem

So now I sail all night to find them and their symbols, to
connect with them whatever seems appropriate, their rings,
their eyes, their ways: but not alone to find the persons
but to find the meanings of the persons to myself, the electric
mind, before the king should claim them from my life.

THE THIN DISEASE

Nearly seven feet tall, a skeleton
made of giant bird bones,
a bird-cage rib-cage,
his heart a little pulsing
robin, Kwame from Ghana
on the old Gold Coast
was my best friend.

Kwame had to reach down
to tap me on my red head. "Dutch,
we're going to cadge some drinks.
You do the talking.
Tell them I'm King Quazi
of oilrich offshore Quaziland,
and I can't speak English.
Tell them my kingdom is ten miles long
and a quarter mile wide, including beaches."

Kwame had purple-grey skin
and was so thin he looked like the shadow of a pole,
but his head was large and noble,
with cheekbones carved in slate,
and royally crested with a pompadour
befitting the son of a son of a king
from the ancient West African Empire,
though he was always church-mouse poor.

We worked on the New York docks,
off-loading ships, on-loading trucks.

He wasn't very strong. He drank a lot
and bled from the rectum when he worked.
They had to cut the grapes away.
Like a daddy longlegs and a flat red beetle,
we wobbled to a bar near St. Vincent's,
a knot of stitches still in his new tight ass.
He could ignore the pain for the booze.

He put his arm over my shoulder.
"Dutch, I'm going to die.
I've got the thin disease.
I'll never go back to Ghana."
"Sure you will. You'll go back."
There were good times yet.
But he died. He died.
He died. The white bed
was empty but for a wave-crested,
welted head, and limp hoses,
some of which were black
and leaked their fluids.
Ghana was far away, a dream,
but I was there, near, here,
his friend, holding his hand,
our funny different fingers
entwined, though pulling apart.

HOPE AND THE BIPOLAR POET

O make me at last an Immortal born for this life,
so hard when the wind like a horse that has eaten of loco weed
kicks in the shining green meadow of death that is the bright day
beyond which the galaxies turn in dark matter like great carousels
with mad imagery rising and falling along their white ways,
all celestial combustion and anger as if there were truth in the gods
and I had come from their birth to mine that happened in heat
in the bowels of the ship of the universe powered by diamonds,
dead glitters of light burnt in the sky. O Heraclitean Fire,
forgive one who has not known the one pinch of peace
held in the index and thumb of the chef who concocted this stew,
brew that biology seeks in its crystals that fall like the fall of each phylum
down the great day of time, no matter all time be an infinite cloud,
O Fire have mercy and snuff out the wick of your running black wax
and spare me the waste of beginnings, evolutions, and ends.

Stop, for the fire at the center of self is the fire at all distances,
emanation and flow like the oceans of life serve likewise the
Heraclitean
Fire
though the walking world is of mercury sulphur and salt, sex sun
and sand,
yet the fire heats the shards till they melt, reshaping themselves in their
clay and
thereby a new entity is formed bearing the heart's evergreen
name of Hope.

CHRONICLE

Out of the mustard tang that filled my mouth
with the vivid day once when wind
brought itself riffling through my short golden mane
like the hand of God being the cub's mother's tongue
came that time when life was endless wonder
and listening to the wind take away laughter
as a chime with wings as little silver
stars afloat like darting butterflies
as sipping hummingbirds at one long meal
within that wind on such wide wings
as monarchs never know nor hummingbirds
but boys and girls flying their youth
wantonly was my dear time wasted
and now it is bells for a stopped watch
where I have ground my teeth out
my novel of ten thousand pages
empty as my mouth.

IV

NOW, THE FOX!

A thousand times I've had this urban dream and
asked a doctor what it meant
　to no avail. "It was the city's grip on
an impressionable child,"
　one doctor told me. I was dropped once down a
hellish, pitch-black pit, a deep
　dumbwaiter shaft, and fell a floor before I
landed, more or less intact.
　I bear a scar above my eye. Could that be
it, dropped by a drunken man,
　a family friend, when I was still an infant?
Meaning harmlessly to play,
　he swore off drink, I'm told. In any case I
have these nightmares constantly,
　and doubt if they will ever go away. Waking,
after one, I'm shaken to
　the bone. I live now in the country, where I
hoped to find diminishment
　of terror, over time. But here's the strange part:
rabies is a major threat
　here in the country in the summer—dogs and
cats can get it from the wild-
　life teeming in the woods—and just the other
night I dreamed a foaming fox
　that chased me back into the cityscape I
hoped so much to free myself
　from, years before, by coming to the country.
Waking horror brought me new
　concern for peace of mind and where to find it.

HEART FAILURE

I have made my moon landing at night
by way of the emergency ward,
on the strong black arm of a nurse.
My wife is the other woman,
and between the two women I enter,
seeing, reflected in glass, my red car
half up on a curb, and mal-angled,
the glare of the high beams showing
my terrified wife's confusion.

There is no air in that car,
there is no air in the night,
but there is air in the hose that the nurse
claps to my turning-blue face,
and strength in her arms that are used to
the harsh struggles that have plagued her existence,
strength that I finally can share in.

I lie in a gown in a room,
and the silent killer says nothing.
He signalled, I guess, with red flags.
I paid no attention. I'd developed
an elephant's hide, an armor for the arrows
of insult that poor boys endure.
From childhood, when I was raw,
and my nerves could actually bleed,
I worked on this suit of armor,
oiled it and flexed it and shined it,
but now it belonged to them,

the doctors who probed me with wonder.
"Didn't you notice a thing?
You sound like a sidewinder, rattling."
"I thought I'd caught cold in the chest."
But I had no desire to know
because I had no desire to stop.
I could see that they thought, "What a fool!"
All but the black nurse, who knew
how the poor slid the slippery slope
that poverty, stress, and high blood pressure
grade for the struggling-upward.
She pulled at my ear, and said, "Tough guy!
He don't take no crap from his heart."
She knew how the pressure builds up,
as you climb in the ignorant ghetto,
until you would break, or be broken.

"How you doing, baby doll? Better?"
"Yes, but now I'm embarrassed."
—embarrassed at being so weak,
ashamed of my heart that can fail,
ashamed to have such a heart—
no lionheart, no Coreleone, I.
But they tell me it's stress that's at fault:
the heart is okay, the tests show.
The angel nurse flattens my hair,
pulls at my ear, and says, "Go!—"

THOSE WHO DIE IN THEIR SLEEP

When the mind is wakeful
and the eyes are shut,
ears buried in their pillows
hear the song and
then it fades behind them
as on a distant shore,
and some drown then
and can never hear again
the song of the dreaming mind
singing its own mystery,
but now the song of the non-
life of the non-mind, of
the stars wheeling to Nowhere,
of time ending, snuffing out
the stars, one by one, the song
of all that has never known
of its own existence.

OLD ICARUS

Grandchildren turning
their faces from
drooling kisses
to avoid
what you have
become:
teeth like graveyard
stones, sunken cheeks
pockmarked
(where once,
as a boy,
the feathers went),
wens, wild hairs.

The wax your father poured
has melted
and the feathers,
plumes he placed so carefully,
flew, fell,
and you fell
into the sea
but did not drown,
owning a future,
as you did,
long enough
to hug your grandchildren
close and have them
turn away.

THE BOP

> *. . . something . . . eternally gained*
> *for the universe . . .*
> —*William James*

I.

When Chips left the Old School he wore its tie
and was carried out with his Wellingtons on.
But no way Doctor Bop, the Burnt-Out Prof.
Things definitely ain't what they used to be.
Bop gets to retire on something like a 401(k);
but not yet, as St. Augustine put it, not quite yet;
I'm not ready for retired sainthood yet!
The syllogisms from which Aristotle deduced the valid
are not complete. In American institutions
we fail upward to glory, and I expect
to be the mad head of the English Department before
I wallop my last tennis ball to cardiac arrest,
or do my last imitation of Johnny Weissmuller.
"Thanotopsis" is *not* my favorite poem.

II.

Old Duracell, old Mazda-man
you've got to keep the light—
it's growing dim inside you
but that's no time to hide you—
there's just a chance you might
say something shedding light.

Old Candle-wick, old Burnt-out Prof,
(who calls himself the Bop)
old hairy ears and snout,
Tochis afn tish!
you gouty worn-out lout—
oh, call yourself a name, old cuss—
because you weren't the best,
and yet you know it doesn't matter,
no, not in the least.

Old geeze, don't lose your grip,
don't fall and break your hip—
you've got to keep the light, baldspot,
you've got to keep the light,
because there's just a chance
if you keep the light, old souse,
if you keep the light,
there's still a chance, though mad,
that there's something left to add.

You've got to keep the light, old piles,
you've got to keep the light.
You know you've been a dog,
oh, you've acted like a *trayf* old hog,
but somehow in your life
you've had a loving wife,
so there must be something good about you,
you lousy lucky lout you—
all I ask of you, old candle,
is just to keep the Godblessed light,
and show a flash of pluck, old duck,
and with a bit of luck
you might come up with something
worthy of the world that you've surveyed.

You've been around so long now
you've got to hold some light,
whether hell or heaven
is waiting with its leaven
to galvanize you new again
for better or for worse,
old man of steel, who once pumped iron,
don't listen to that deathly siren,
you've got to keep the light a while,
you've got to keep that gap-toothed smile,
you've got to keep the light alive
inside your horrible old hide,
because you still might do a thing
that's worthy of its doing,
you've got to keep the light, old pipe,
you've got to keep the light.

You've written many a poem, old bard,
and published many too,
but I've got news for you, old prof,
I've got news for you—
you haven't any right, old cough,
not to keep the light.
You don't get off like that, old shakes
fall off the roof like that—
there's plenty time to die, old guy,
plenty time to die,
so keep on pumping light, old Bop,
pumping students light!

OLD CHORISTERS

Singers
of our generation
are turning up
dead. A serial
killer
is injecting
them
with cancer
heart disease
and stroke.
This police
silhouette
of the killer
isn't made
of his head,
but of his
twisted mind,
made
of a brain
to answer
for his crimes
of torture
perpetrated
on so many
choristers.
With a rough
cat-tongue
he licked flesh
from bones
and made

the other
mercy-kill
to make
amends.
Look,
from
a high bridge,
as highway god,
he drops
stones on old bones!
Even the sap
of trees is worried
up the trunk
as the killer
waits
for an autumnal
weariness of
leaves.
I am
Time's agent
his tool
he brags.
Singers
of our generation
think that this
is a serial crime,
but have
no choice
but to
become ringers
and to pull
the ropes
and toll
the bell

BECAUSE

in the port-cities they have found everything out and
Aristotle-like have put everything into categories
and the unicorn is an ungulate because they say so
because the fine-print of the unreligious sun says we circle it
it is not for us but we for it because the moon hit us
and bounced off instead of was born of our first spin
because the ninth planet is an invading comet caught
and because there is no now and there never has been

because we look upon ourselves in savannas past
knuckling to water because we see the white lemming's hole
in the snow smashed down by hooves and hear its pitiful
chirp of counter-aggression because the avalanche
indifferently buries the contested world of the snow
valley because stars die because we believe in facts
and because the deluge led to the ark because because
and because we bury our dead and dig up their bones

because the unsoundness of our judgments lead to sound
judgment and because facts are facts and we must reckon
and because the sea is cruel and because time flies
because the wind blows down our houses and because
we remember the snow hare and the hawk because
because the dove is taken in air by the eagle
and because space is either empty or full of dark matter
because galaxies hold for a long time their pinwheel-shapes

because time and space are curved and we can blow ourselves up
and because we blow ourselves up constantly and because

it makes us wonder because doesn't it mean something
because we are riding a mud-ball through space because
we were born here and because we have categories and
because we dig up our bones and dogs dig our bones up
and because we are not even safe in pyramids because
we dig ourselves up and look upon our own bones